CONTENTS

Bunny Bed Set, Quilted Cornice, Bunny Lamp, Child's Brush Set

Victorian Basinette Set, Rosebud and Teddy Crib Set, Nursery Lamp, Painted Accessories, Painted Mother's Rocker, Little Angel Shelf, Baby's Rug, Roses and Ribbon Basket

Pink Violets Towel Set, Pillows, Bath Rug, Painted Lace Shelf Skirt, Guest Towels, Decorative Pillow

English Rose Potpourri, Pomander, Nursery Potpourri, Lavender Bunny, Victorian Kitchen Potpourri, Victorian Spice Potpourri, Wall Sachet

CREDITS: JONI PRITTIE: DESIGNER, ARTIST. TODD TSUKUSHI: PHOTOGRAPHY. IRENE MORRIS: GRAPHIC DESIGN.
MANY THANKS TO: APPLE LANE BED AND BREAKFAST INN, APTOS, CA., THE BAYVIEW HOTEL, APTOS, CA.,
GOSBY HOUSE INN, PACIFIC GROVE, CA., GREEN GABLES BED AND BREAKFAST INN, PACIFIC GREOVE, CA., GREY DOVE, CAPITOLA, CA.,
SMITH'S CHINA SHOP, SANTA CRUZ, CA.

© 1990 JONI PRITTIE   PRINTED IN HONG KONG

FLORAL PILLOWS

MATERIALS COST: $5-$10   APPROXIMATE TIME TO CREATE: 30 MINUTES

Create a Victorian mood with accent pillows. Plain purchased pillows, fused or appliqued with florals from the skirt table print are the coordinating touch in this setting.

SUPPLIES

2 READY MADE PILLOWS—
ONE HEART SHAPED AND
ONE OBLONG

1/4 YD. FLORAL FABRIC

1/4 YD. FUSIBLE WEB

SQUEEZE BOTTLE FABRIC
PAINTS—IRIDESCENT ROSE,
GREEN AND CRYSTAL
GLITTERING

CARE REMINDER:

Custom made fused pieces are more delicate and must have special washing care. Hand washing is best, but fused things will tolerate machine washings in cool water. Hang items to air dry. Any fused edges that loosen can be easily secured with washable fabric glue.

OBLONG PILLOW

STEP 1

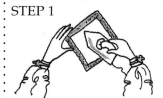

Iron fusible web to wrong-side of printed fabric under three flower sprays.

STEP 2

Cut out flower and leaf shapes. Peel away paper backing.

STEP 3

Fuse flower sprays to pillow center as shown.

STEP 4
Paint around stems and flower shapes with free flowing strokes.

HEART PILLOW

Simply follow steps for oblong pillow, but rather than cutting individual flowers, cut a heart shape from print and fuse to pillow. Fuse two tiny flowers or leaves to pillow, overlapping into heart. Dot glittering paint around heart edge for beaded effect.

VICTORIAN FAN
FIRE SCREEN

MATERIALS COST $25-$35   APPROXIMATE TIME TO CREATE: 1 HOUR

*ans of all kinds appear in the Victorian home.
A marbled paper fan serves to back our floral arrangement and
hide an unused fire box.*

SUPPLIES

1 PURCHASED PAPER
FIRE SCREEN FAN

1 BLOCK DRIED
FLOWER OASIS

1 LARGE HANDFUL
FLORIST MOSS

7 LARGE PAPER ZINNIAS,
PLUM, RUST AND ROSE

2 PEACH SILK IRISES

3 SPRAYS PALE PEACH
SILK FREESIAS

1 STEM PINK SILK
SWEET PEAS

1 STEM MAUVE SILK
SWEET PEAS

2 STEMS PEACH SILK
FORSYTHIA

5 STEMS TINY PINK AND
WHITE PAPER BLOSSOMS

1 BUNCH DRIED LAVENDER

GLUE GUN/GLUE STICKS

STEP 1
Cover oasis block with florist
moss. Secure moss with hot glue.

STEP 2
Arrange small paper flowers,
freesias and forsythia first. This
will give fullness and shape to
the arrangement.

STEP 3
Place larger flowers as shown
and fill in with lavender stems
and medium sized flowers.

TIP: Scent silk and paper flower arrangements by adding a cotton ball soaked in scented oil to
florist moss.

VICTORIAN BELL PULL

MATERIALS COST: $10-$15   APPROXIMATE TIME TO CREATE: 30 MINUTES

ell pulls were quite essential in the large Victorian home.
A simple pull summoned a cup of tea for the lady of the house.
Alas, ours is purely ornamental.

SUPPLIES

6 INCH X 24 INCH PIECE
PEACH SILK MOIRE

3 1/2 INCH X 24 INCH PLAIN
COTTON FOR BACKING

4 SMALL FLORAL SPRAYS
FROM PRINTED COTTON

2 TINY BERRY SPRIGS FROM
PRINTED COTTON

1/4 YD. FUSIBLE WEB

1 1/2 YD. 1/4 INCH
GOLD BRAID OR TRIM

SQUEEZE BOTTLE FABRIC
PAINT—GLITTERY GOLD

1 SET GOLD EMBROIDERED
APPLIQUES

1 6 INCH CREAM
SILK TASSLE

GLUE GUN/GLUE STICK

STEP 1

Fold and glue moire strip as
shown.

STEP 2

Iron fusible web to wrong-side
of cotton backing fabric. Peel
away paper backing and fuse
strip to back of bell pull.

STEP 3
Following instructions on inside
back cover, fuse flower and
berry sprays to front of bell pull
as shown.

STEP 4
Glue gold braid trim down both
sides of bell pull, approximately
1/8 inch from edge.

STEP 5
Glue gold appliques to top and
bottom end and tie or glue tassle
to bell pull end.

PICTURE BOWS

MATERIALS COST: $5-$10   APPROXIMATE TIME TO CREATE: 20 MINUTES

asy as can be, bows add Victorian flair to framed paintings, photos and trinket collections.

Lockets, Grandmother's music pin and a few pressed flowers mounted on woven cotton are displayed in a simple frame. Use 1 inch wide deep plum ribbon over 1 3/4 inch wide teal ribbon for bow and streamer.

This bow takes 1 yd. each ribbon.

Variegated silk ribbon is the key to this delicate look.

This bow takes 1 yd. rainbow silk ribbon.

Copy flower colors used in the framed print to add dimension to picture bow glued to top center of frame.

This bow takes 1/2 yd. grey wire edge ribbon, two sprigs baby's breath and just a few tiny, dried pink flowers.

Picture bows are decorative. Paintings and framed prints are actually supported on wall with a picture hanger attached to frame.

STEP 1

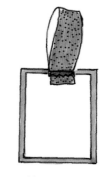

Form a ribbon loop and glue to top center of frame back.

STEP 2

Make a single or double bow and glue to loop as shown.

STEP 3

Glue streamer pieces to back side of frame as shown. Length of streamers will be determined by frame size.

TOPIARY

MATERIALS COST: $5-$10   APPROXIMATE TIME TO CREATE: 30 MINUTES

lder, English gardens are graced with the most wonderful topiaries shaped into birds, animals and lovely geometric shapes. Make this tiny topiary and dream of an English garden.

SUPPLIES

1 3 INCH STYROFOAM™ BALL

HANDFUL GREEN FLORIST MOSS

1 LONG STEM TINY LAVENDER PAPER FLOWERS

1 5 INCH TREE TWIG

1 4 INCH CLAY FLOWERPOT

1 PIECE OASIS TO FIT IN FLOWERPOT

HANDFUL GREY-GREEN MOSS

CRAFT PAINT— COLONIAL GREEN

SEA SPONGE

1/4 INCH VARIEGATED SILK RIBBON—1 INCH WIDE

CRAFT GLUE

STEP 1
Cover styrofoam™ ball with craft glue and pat on green moss to cover completely.

STEP 2
Mix craft paint with equal amount water and pat paint on flowerpot with sponge. Allow clay color to show through.

STEP 3
Push twig into moss covered ball. Place oasis in flowerpot and push twig end securely into oasis.

STEP 4
Add grey-green moss to topiary base.

STEP 5
Spiral long paper flower stem around tree, securing by pushing wire ends into foam.

STEP 6
Tie a single bow and glue to flowerpot rim.

TIP: Make a scented topiary by substituting potpourri for green moss. Simply roll glued ball in potpourri.

COVERED PHOTO ALBUM

MATERIALS COST: $10-$15   APPROXIMATE TIME TO CREATE: 1 HOUR

Keep treasured family memories close at hand, beautifully presented...

SUPPLIES

1 PHOTO ALBUM

1/2 YD. PAISLEY POLISHED COTTON

1/2 YD. LIGHT WEIGHT COTTON BATTING

1/4 YD. GOLD BRAID

1 SMALL GOLD BELL

1 READY MADE DESIGNER TASSLE

2 YD. NAVY WOVEN RIBBON

GLUE GUN/GLUE STICKS

STEP 1

Glue sections of cotton batting to front and back of album.

STEP 2

Lay album flat and cut fabric as shown.

STEP 3

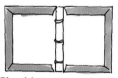

Glue fabric to cover book as shown. Tuck tab into album spine and glue in place.

STEP 4

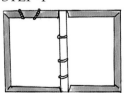

Glue gold braid to top, inside front cover as shown.

STEP 5

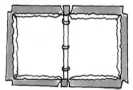

Glue ribbon around fabric edges on inside covers.

STEP 6

Tie bell and tassle to gold cord.

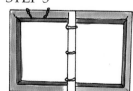

PAISLEY PILLOWS

MATERIALS COST: $10-$20   APPROXIMATE TIME TO CREATE: 45 MINUTES

V

elvet, polished cotton and glittery gold edging combine for a rich Victorian look.

SUPPLIES

1 15 INCH NAVY VELVET PILLOW

1 15 INCH HUNTER GREEN VELVET PILLOW

1/2 YD. PAISLEY POLISHED COTTON

1/2 YD. FUSIBLE WEB

SQUEEZE BOTTLE FABRIC PAINT—GLITTERY PLATINUM GOLD

STEP 1

Following instructions on inside back cover, fuse web to paisley fabric.

STEP 2

Cut out large paisley shapes. Peel away paper backing.

STEP 3

Fuse designs to pillow centers, using tip of iron. Be careful to iron on cotton only, as heat may damage velvet.

STEP 4

Outline all shapes with fabric paint.

DECORATIVE
SCENTED FAN

MATERIALS COST: $3-$5   APPROXIMATE TIME TO CREATE: 20 MINUTES

Perfume the air with a small Victorian fan...displayed on your tabletop or as a wall decoration.

SUPPLIES

Fan can be purchased scented or apply scented oil to wood sections of fan.

1 8 INCH GREEN PAPER FAN

3/4 YD. 1/4 INCH CREAM SATIN RIBBON

6 TINY PAPER BLACK BERRIES

5 TINY DRIED WHITE FLOWERS

1 TINY DRIED PINK FLOWER

3 SPRIGS PRESERVED BABY'S BREATH

2 SMALL SPRIGS GREEN SILK LEAVES

GLUE GUN/GLUE STICKS

STEP 1
Glue a tiny bouquet of flowers and leaves on right-side of fan. Tuck baby's breath and berries to fill out shape.

STEP 2
Tie a small triple bow and glue to fan as shown. Trim streamers to six inches.

HEARTS AND FLOWERS BOX

MATERIALS COST: $5-$7 APPROXIMATE TIME TO CREATE: 30 MINUTES

ifts for dear friends or simply treasures to keep, covered boxes are surprisingly simple to make. Floral prints and stripe prints work well. This project is perfect for small scraps of fabrics.

SUPPLIES

1 HEART SHAPED WOOD BOX

1/4 YD. FLORAL PRINTED FABRIC

1/2 YD STRIP BORDER PRINT

1/2 YD. FUSIBLE WEB

1/4 YD. 3 INCH WIDE FLAT LACE

7 SMALL GREEN SILK LEAVES

1 SPRIG DRIED GERMAN STATICE

3 SMALL DRIED PINK FLOWERS

4 SINGLE BABY'S BREATH FLOWERS

1 MEDIUM PINK PORCELAIN ROSE

2 SMALL PINK PORCELAIN ROSES

SQUEEZE-BOTTLE FABRIC PAINTS—LIGHT GREEN, PEARL PINK, AND PEARL CREAM

PENCIL

FABRIC GLUE

GLUE GUN/GLUE STICKS

STEP 1
Fuse web to reverse-side of printed and border print fabrics, following instructions on inside back cover.

STEP 2
Lay box top on floral fabric and draw around box shape with pencil or fabric pen. Cut out shape, peel off paper backing and fuse to box top with iron set on a medium setting. Fusing takes beautifully on wood. Trim any excess fabric away.

STEP 3
Cut strip of border print and fuse to box, using the tip of your iron. Trim any excess fabric away.

STEP 4
Lay box bottom section on floral fabric and mark width. Roll box slightly to get a second marking place and draw straight line. Cut out strip and fuse to box. Trim away any excess fabric.

STEP 5
Cut a strip of lace to lay diagonally across box top. Glue and trim away excess lace.

STEP 6
Glue green leaves to box and arrange sprigs of dried flowers. Glue on three porcelain roses.

TIP: Make thoughtful occasion boxes by simply using holiday fabrics. Covered boxes add both grace and function to the bedroom and dressing room...a lovely hiding place for pins and hair barrettes.

TIP: Scent your boxes by simply gluing a few potpourri petals to the floral decorations.

LITTLE SWEETHEART BOX

ictorian boxes are a perfect accent for the dining room—or any room of your house. They also make perfect homemade gifts for the holidays.

SUPPLIES

1 HEART SHAPED WOODEN BOX

1/8 YD. FLORAL PRINTED FABRIC

1/8 YD. FUSIBLE WEB

3/4 YD. EACH—MINT AND PINK 1/4 INCH WIDE RIBBON

4 SMALL GREEN SILK LEAVES

1 SPRIG DRIED GERMAN STATICE

3 SMALL DRIED BLUE FLOWERS

4 SPRIGS BABY'S BREATH FLOWERS

3 PINK PORCELAIN CARNATIONS

2 SMALL SPRIGS PINK BERRIES

1 SMALL CRANBERRY BIRD IN HER NEST

SQUEEZE BOTTLE FABRIC PAINTS—IRIDESCENT GREEN, WHITE AND PINK, CRYSTAL

PENCIL

FABRIC GLUE

GLUE GUN/GLUE STICKS

STEP 1
Fuse web to reverse-side of print, following instructions on inside back cover.

STEP 2
Lay box top on floral fabric and draw around box shape with pencil or fabric pen. Cut out shape, peel off paper backing and fuse to box top with iron set on a medium setting. Fusing takes beautifully on wood. Trim any excess fabric with scissors.

STEP 3
Cut strip of fabric and fuse to box sides using the tip of your iron. Trim any excess fabric away.

STEP 4
Lay box bottom section on floral fabric and mark width. Roll box slightly to get a second marking place and draw straight line. Cut out strip and fuse to box. Trim away any excess fabric.

STEP 5
Paint squiggles and dots around outside edge of box top. Allow paint to dry completely.

STEP 6
Glue green and pink ribbons to box sides and dot ribbons with alternate color paints. Allow paint to dry.

STEP 7
Glue a little bird and nest in place. Glue flowers and leaves around bird. Add a single pink bow.

TIP: Gifts and holidays are perfect uses for small covered boxes. Simply substitute holiday fabrics and add trim.

TIP: Store potpourri in wooden boxes for a few weeks. The wood will become scented.

ELEGANT DINING CLOTH

MATERIALS COST: $10–$20   APPROXIMATE TIME TO CREATE: 1 HOUR

*T*reasured linens of yesteryear set the stage for romantic evening meals. Create your own heirlooms—linens made to your color scheme. The light, airy mood of white sparkles with the addition of fresh green and peach printed cotton. Lilies of the valley, often grandmother's favorite flower, add Victorian charm.

SUPPLIES

1 LARGE WHITE OVAL TABLECLOTH

1/4 YD. LILY OF THE VALLEY PRINT

1/2 YD. PEACH FLORAL PRINT

1/4 YD. IVY PRINT

1 YD. FUSIBLE WEB

SQUEEZE-BOTTLE FABRIC PAINT—WHITE

CARE REMINDER:

Custom made fused pieces are more delicate and must have special washing care. Hand washing is best, but fused things will tolerate machine washings in cool water. Hang items to air dry. Any fused edges that loosen can be easily secured with washable fabric glue.

STEP 1

Following instructions on inside back cover, fuse web to printed fabrics.

STEP 2

Cut out all flower, ivy and leaf shapes. Peel away paper backings.

STEP 3

Fuse flowers, ivy and leaves to form a center oval, as shown in photograph. Fuse small floral groupings around hem as shown.

STEP 4

Paint white squiggles around designs to create the feeling of embroidery.

ELEGANT NAPKIN RINGS

MATERIALS COST: $5-10   APPROXIMATE TIME TO CREATE: 1 HOUR

ade simply of moire ribbon and fabric scraps, these elegant napkin rings complete a very special setting.

SUPPLIES

1 YD. 2 1/2 INCH WIDE GREEN MOIRE RIBBON—NON-WOVEN

1/4 YD. WHITE COTTON FABRIC

4 SMALL SPRAYS OF FLOWERS USED IN TABLECLOTH

1/2 YD. FUSIBLE WEB

FABRIC STIFFENER

SQUEEZE-BOTTLE FABRIC PAINTS: IRIDESCENT PEACH, IRIDESCENT CREAM AND GREEN

2 YD. TINY PEARL TRIM

GLUE GUN/GLUE STICKS

ROLLING PIN

ALUMINUM FOIL

STEP 1

Cut ribbon in four 8 inch lengths. Cut fusible web in strips to fit exactly on ribbon back. Fuse web to ribbon backs but **do not** peel away paper backing.

STEP 2

Fuse web to wrong-side of four flower sprays. Cut out flower shapes and peel away paper backings.

STEP 3

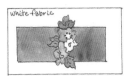

Peel away fusible paper backing from ribbon. Lay ribbon lengths on white fabric. Position flower shapes on center portion of ribbon, allowing tips or leaves of flowers to overlap ribbon. Since both ribbon and flower shapes have fusible web, one simple ironing process will bind both ribbon and flower tips to white cloth. Fuse ribbon and flowers by simply ironing.

STEP 4

Trim around ribbon and flower tips. The entire surface will be backed with white fabric.

STEP 5

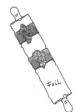

Shape ribbon section to form a circle with floral designs on top. Overlap ribbon ends and secure with glue gun.

STEP 6

Apply fabric stiffener to inside surface of ring. Cover rolling pin with aluminum foil. Slide stiffened napkin rings on rolling pin to dry. This will hold their form. Allow to dry completely. Remove stiff napkin rings from rolling pin.

NOTE: These napkin rings are not washable.

STEP 7
Detail flowers and leaves with fabric paint.

STEP 8
Glue tiny pearls on edges of napkin rings.

VICTORIAN LACE CENTERPIECE

SEE INDIVIDUAL MATERIALS LISTS FOR TIME AND MATERIALS COSTS.

SUPPLIES FOR LACE CENTERPIECE

1 18 INCH ROUND WHITE LACE FABRIC

1 YD. 1 INCH WIDE RUFFLED WHITE LACE

1 YD. 2 1/2 INCH WIDE RUFFLED WHITE LACE

1 1/2 YD. 1 1/2 INCH WIDE GREEN MOIRE RIBBON—NON-WOVEN

FABRIC STIFFENER

LIGHT CARDBOARD—14 INCH SQUARE

ALUMINUM FOIL

RUBBER BAND

GLUE GUN/GLUE STICKS

MATERIALS COST: $5-$10

APPROXIMATE TIME TO CREATE: 1 HOUR

SUPPLIES FOR BOUQUET

2 LARGE SILK TULIPS

3 MEDIUM SILK BLOSSOMS

3 SPRIGS TINY SILK BLOSSOMS

1 SMALL BUNCH GERMAN STATICE

3 STEMS DRIED LARKSPUR

2 LARGE SILK ROSES

1 SMALL BUNCH BABY'S BREATH

WIRE CUTTER

FLORIST TAPE

MATERIALS COST: $10-$25

APPROXIMATE TIME TO CREATE: 20 MINUTES

Victorian lace and flowers accent our table. Flowers are dried and silk, combined in colors and textures to compliment the room, all tied in lace and ribbon...the feeling of a garden bouquet just gathered. Easy to make, the lace bouquet is a larger version of the Victorian tussie-mussie. Lace is stiffened to hold the shape. Bouquets can be changed according to the season.

LACE CENTERPIECE INSTRUCTIONS

STEP 1
Form a cone with cardboard. Cover cone with aluminum foil.

STEP 2
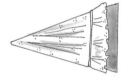

Dip lace in fabric stiffener. Press stiffener into cloth for complete saturation. Place wet lace over cone and mold to create a lace cone shape. Secure with rubber band. Allow to dry and harden completely before removing from cone.

STEP 3
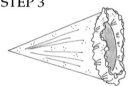

Glue 2 1/2 inch lace to inner hem of lace opening, with lace facing as shown. Glue 1 inch lace on outer hem edges of cone.

STEP 4

Trim a 16 inch length of ribbon to 1 inch width. Glue around lace as shown.

STEP 5

Tie a single bow of full-width ribbon and glue to ribbon seam.

BOUQUET INSTRUCTIONS

STEP 1
Cut wire stems to 6 inch lengths. Use a mix of dried and silk flowers to form small florets. Florist tape will stick as it is stretched. Twist tape around stems.

STEP 2
Mix silk and dried flowers and continue adding flowers and twisting tape around stems until 12 inch round bouquet is formed. Place in lace cone.

TEA ^{FOR} TWO LINEN SET

Cherries and garden blossoms give the feeling of cheer, a reminder of the seasons of the garden.

SUPPLIES FOR TABLE RUNNER

1 WHITE LINEN TABLE RUNNER WITH BATTENBURG LACE TRIM

1/4 YD. FABRIC WITH FLORAL AND CHERRY PRINT

1/4 YD. FUSIBLE WEB

MATERIALS COST: $2-$5

APPROXIMATE TIME TO CREATE: 20 MINUTES

INSTRUCTIONS FOR TABLE RUNNER

Following instructions on inside back cover (also shown here), and fuse small sprigs of flowers and cherries to table runner as shown, fuse designs over embroidery if necessary, as we have done.

STEP 1	STEP 2	STEP 3

Iron on fusible webbing to wrong-side of fabric.	*Cut out design, peel away paper backing.*	*Iron design onto item.*

SUPPLIES FOR MUFFIN BASKET CLOTH

1 WHITE LINEN BREAD CLOTH

1 SMALL SCRAP FABRIC WITH FLORAL AND CHERRY PRINT

1 SMALL SCRAP FUSIBLE WEB

MATERIALS COST: $.50-$1

APPROXIMATE TIME TO CREATE: 10 MINUTES

Simply follow instructions on inside front cover and fuse a tiny flower or cherry sprig to corners of bread cloth.

SUPPLIES FOR CHERRY LINEN DOILY

1 5 INCH DOILY WITH BATTENBURG LACE TRIM

1 SMALL SCRAP FABRIC WITH PRINTED CHERRIES

1 SMALL SCRAP FUSIBLE WEB

MATERIALS COST: $.50-$1

APPROXIMATE TIME TO CREATE: 10 MINUTES

Follow instructions on inside front cover and simply fuse one sprig of cherries to cloth center.

CARE REMINDER:

Custom made fused pieces are more delicate and must have special washing care. Hand washing is best, but fused things will tolerate machine washings in cool water. Hang items to air dry. Any fused edges that loosen can be easily secured with washable fabric glue.

FLORAL
KEEPSAKE DOME

MATERIALS COST: $5-$10   APPROXIMATE TIME TO CREATE: 20 MINUTES

ictorian glass domes display butterflies and collections of natural objects. Our dome evokes the feeling of peeking into a wooded glen.

SUPPLIES

1 11 INCH GLASS DOME

1 WALNUT BASE TO FIT THE DOME

1 2 INCH ROUND FLORIST FOAM

HANDFUL FLORIST MOSS

2 SMALL TWIGS FROM THE GARDEN

1 SPRIG GERMAN STATICE

1 STEM PAPER FLOWERS— AMARANTH WAS USED HERE

1 STEM DRIED PURPLE LARKSPUR

1 STEM DRIED PINK LARKSPUR

1 TINY SPRIG BABY'S BREATH

1 TINY SPRIG DRIED TANSY

GLUE GUN/GLUE STICKS

STEP 1

Secure foam to center of wooden base with glue. Pat moss all around and secure in places with glue.

STEP 2

Push twigs into foam and arrange flowers and leaves to form a tall, narrow shape. Check often to see if dome fits over completed arrangement.

BOUQUET OF ROSES PICTURE

MATERIALS COST: $5-$8   APPROXIMATE TIME TO CREATE: 1 HOUR

*B*askets of fragrant roses are never out of season. An oval framed fabric collage above the mantle, brings fresh dimension and color to the room. Colors taken from the wallpaper and room fabrics blend to make the perfect accent piece for our Victorian tea party.

SUPPLIES

1 LARGE GOLD OVAL FRAME—OURS IS 18 X 23 INCHES

MEDIUM WEIGHT CARD-BOARD, CUT TO FIT IN FRAME

1/2 YD. ROSE AND WHITE STRIPED COTTON

1/4 YD. GREEN CALICO PRINT

1/2 YD. 1 1/2 INCH WIDE PRINTED RIBBON

1 SQUARE COTTON PRINTED WITH VICTORIAN FLOWER BASKET

1/4 YD. SMALL FLORAL PRINT WITH CHERRIES AND FLOWERS

1 SMALL SCRAP PAISLEY PRINTED FABRIC

1 7 INCH WHITE LINEN DOILY WITH BATTENBURG LACE TRIM

2 YD. FUSIBLE WEB

SQUEEZE-BOTTLE FABRIC PAINTS—IRIDESCENT BLUE, IRIDESCENT ROSE, DARK GREEN AND PINK

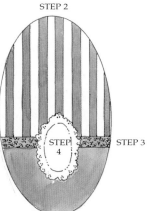

STEP 2

STEP 3

STEP 4

STEP 5

STEP 1
Fuse web to wrong-side of striped fabric, calico, ribbon and floral pieces, paisleys and doily center.

STEP 2
Fuse background fabrics to cardboard.

STEP 3
Fuse printed ribbon to cover seams of background fabrics.

STEP 4
Fuse doily to picture as shown. Fuse flower basket portion of print on doily. Fuse cherries and sprigs of flowers to give a full effect.

STEP 5
Paint flower, leaf, and basket edges with flowing strokes. Add paint details to flower centers and basket.

STEP 6
Trim away any excess fabric from oval and fit picture into frame.

VICTORIAN BASKET TABLERUNNER

MATERIALS COST: $5-$10   APPROXIMATE TIME TO CREATE: 15 MINUTES

*O**ur white linen table runner began life as a dresser cloth. Fuse blue and white printed baskets down the center for a crisp, country Victorian look.***

SUPPLIES

1 WHITE LINEN OR COTTON TABLE RUNNER

1/2 YD. BLUE AND WHITE PRINT

1/2 YD. FUSIBLE WEB

STEP 1

Following instructions on inside back cover, fuse web to printed fabric.

STEP 2

Cut out large print shapes or baskets. Peel away paper backings.

STEP 3

Fuse shapes or baskets to form a center design, running the length of table runner.

GARDEN HERBS
PICTURE FRAME

MATERIALS COST: $5-$10   APPROXIMATE TIME TO CREATE: 30 MINUTES

Feature a favorite recipe in a frame, covered with fabric to coordinate with your color scheme. Blue and white is the classic combination to complement flowers and food.

SUPPLIES

1 8 X 10 PICTURE MAT

1/4 YD. SMALL CALICO PRINT

1/3 YD. LIGHT COTTON BATTING

1/2 YD. WHITE COTTON EYELET TRIM

DRIED HERBS AND FLOWERS

3 SMALL WHITE SILK BLOSSOMS

FABRIC MARKING PEN

GLUE GUN/GLUE STICKS

STEP 1

Place mat on wrong-side of fabric and draw around mat.

STEP 2

Measure 1 inch around markings and cut as shown.

STEP 3

Glue inside edges to wrong-side of mat.

STEP 4

Cut small strips of batting and place between fabric and mat.

STEP 5

Glue outer edges of fabric to back of mat.

STEP 6

Glue eyelet trim to back of mat as shown.

STEP 7

Glue herbs to mat to form a tiny bouquet. Glue a small scrap of white eyelet to form a bow and add three silk blossoms.

PAINTED GLASSWARE

MATERIALS COST: $5-$10   APPROXIMATE TIME TO CREATE: 20 MINUTES

reasured painted glassware can be copied easily in minutes with the fabric paints that are available in small squeeze bottles. This is truly the most simple craft of all.

SUPPLIES

SMALL ORNAMENTAL
GLASSWARE

SQUEEZE-BOTTLE FABRIC
PAINTS

Painted glassware is not dishwasher safe, but can be easily washed by hand with a light cloth. Wet paint can easily be wiped off, so if a mistake occurs, clean area with tissue.

Paint will dry in about an hour and will be quite durable. If you want to change design, peel dried paint from glass and begin again. This craft works well for Christmas ornaments, decorative glass bowls, candlesticks, or for glass or ceramic lamp bases.

Clean glass thoroughly, use small strokes and dots to create floral or dot designs. Allow paint to dry completely.

IDEAS

- *Paint wine glass party favors for the bride's luncheon.*
- *Clear or colored glass bowls*
- *Kitchen storage jars*
- *Glass candlesticks*
- *Glass or ceramic lamp vases*
- *Decorative plates to display on walls*
- *Vases*
- *Jam jars for special gifts*
- *Decorate windows for special holidays (to remove decorations, scrape with razor blade).*

FRUIT ORCHARD KITCHEN SET

ring out the soft glow of light to your countertop or kitchen desk by adding a small, simple lamp. Print colors come alive when lamp is lit.

SUPPLIES FOR PLACE MATS

Instructions are for two place mats and two napkins

PLAIN COLORED QUILTED PLACE MATS

PLAIN COLORED NAPKINS

1/4 YD. FRUIT PRINT, COTTON

1/4 YD. FUSIBLE WEB

SQUEEZE-BOTTLE FABRIC PAINTS—DARK GREEN, COPPER AND CINNAMON

SUPPLIES FOR NAPKIN RING

1 CARDBOARD PAPER TOWEL OR BATHROOM TISSUE TUBE

1/8 YD. PRINTED FABRIC

1/8 YD. FUSIBLE WEB

SMALL SPRIG DRIED FLOWERS

GLUE GUN/GLUE STICKS

SUPPLIES FOR LAMPSHADE

1 10 INCH BEIGE LAMPSHADE

1/4 YD. FRUIT PRINT, COTTON

1/4 YD. FUSIBLE WEB

SQUEEZE-BOTTLE FABRIC PAINTS—DARK GREEN, COPPER AND CINNAMON

INSTRUCTIONS FOR PLACEMATS

STEP 1
Following instructions on inside back cover, fuse web to printed fabric.

STEP 2
Cut fruit shapes and peel away paper backings.

STEP 3
Fuse designs to place mat. Fuse one small flower to napkin.

STEP 4
Paint around edges and detail designs with fabric paint.

INSTRUCTIONS FOR NAPKIN RINGS

STEP 1

Following instructions on inside front cover, fuse web to printed fabric. Peel away paper backing.

STEP 2

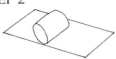

Cut cardboard tube in 2 inch sections. Cut fabric in rectangular shape to allow 1/2 inch overlap at back of ring.

STEP 3

Fuse fabric to cardboard and cut excess fabric as shown. Using iron tip, fuse excess fabric to inside of ring.

STEP 4

Glue small sprigs of dried flowers or herbs to ring.

STEP 5

Form two small single loops of fabric and glue to ring to form bow. Add a tiny piece of fabric to create a bow center, or glue a few dried flowers to bow center.

INSTRUCTIONS FOR LAMPSHADE

STEP 1

Following instructions on inside back cover, fuse web to fabric.

STEP 2
Cut out fruit shapes and peel away paper backings.

STEP 3
Fuse designs to shade. Use a medium heat iron setting.

STEP 4
Paint around edges and detail designs with fabric paint.

AUTUMN BIRDS KITCHEN SET

MATERIALS COST: $3-$5 APPROXIMATE TIME TO CREATE: 20 MINUTES

Teal, gold and autumn rust prints decorate everyday kitchen items found in discount stores. Make one set to keep and one set for a housewarming present...

SUPPLIES

1 QUILTED OVEN MITT

1 QUILTED POT HOLDER

1 KITCHEN TOWEL

1/4 YD. PRINTED COTTON

1/4 YD. FUSIBLE WEB

CARE REMINDER:

Custom made fused pieces are more delicate and must have special washing care. Hand washing is best, but fused things will tolerate machine washings in cool water. Hang items to air dry. Any fused edges that loosen can be easily secured with washable fabric glue.

STEP 1

Following instructions on inside back cover, fuse web to printed fabric.

STEP 2

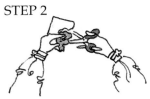

Cut out flowers and bird shapes. Peel away paper backings.

STEP 3

Fuse designs to mitt, towel and pot holder. Iron well to secure shapes to quilted fabrics.

HERB GARDEN WREATH

MATERIALS COST: $10-$15   APPROXIMATE TIME TO CREATE: 1 HOUR

ounties of the kitchen garden make a beautiful and useful kitchen wreath. Dried herbs can be clipped for cooking and garlic buds pinched off for that special sauce. Collect herbs from the garden after dew has evaporated. Hang small bunches to dry. Fresh herbs purchased from the grocery store dry well.

SUPPLIES

1 14 INCH MOSS COVERED WREATH

1 BUNCH DRIED OREGANO

1 BUNCH DRIED ROSEMARY

1 BUNCH DRIED MINT

3 ARTIFICIAL GRAPE BUNCHES

2 STEMS ARTIFICIAL PLUMS

2 STEMS ARTIFICIAL CRAB APPLES

2 STEMS ARTIFICIAL PEAS

3 STEMS PAPER MACHE BERRIES

5 BULBS GARLIC

5 SMALL YELLOW PIECES NATURAL RAFFIA OR THIN PAPER RIBBON

GLUE GUN/GLUE STICKS

STEP 1

Place wreath on flat surface and glue sprigs of dried herbs to front surface of wreath.

STEP 2

Glue fruit and vegetables to wreath.

STEP 3
Tie five single bows of raffia and glue to wreath, tucked in among fruit shapes.

TIP: For a just gathered look, leave root ends on garlic. If your garlic is purchased it may be very clean looking. Simply rub a bit of wet mud on the garlic...it will look homegrown when the mud dries.

HARVEST BASKET

MATERIALS COST: $10-$15   APPROXIMATE TIME TO CREATE: 30 MINUTES

reate this picture perfect centerpiece so easily. Fresh fruit simply placed in our decorative basket sets the mood for any season.

SUPPLIES

1 VICTORIAN SHAPED BASKET

HANDFUL FLORISTS MOSS

1 STEM ARTIFICIAL FRUIT

1 STEM PAPER MACHE RASPBERRIES AND BLACKBERRIES

1 STEM SMALL BERRIES

1 SPRAY BLUE DRIED FLOWERS

GLUE GUN/GLUE STICKS

STEP 1

Glue small pieces of moss all around top edge of basket.

STEP 2

Glue fruit and berries into moss, around basket edge.

STEP 3
Complete basket by simply gluing in tiny pieces of dried flowers among fruit and berries.

Decorate any shape basket using this method. Silk flowers can be substituted for fruit on spring baskets.

VICTORIAN BED SET

MATERIALS COST: $15-$20   APPROXIMATE TIME TO CREATE: 2 HOURS

Peaches and cream, is the theme for our sweet bed set. Decorate a basic bed set, add lace pillows and a decorated lamp shade for a designer look at delightfully small cost.

SUPPLIES

1 PLAIN PEACH QUILTED BEDSPREAD

1 SET PILLOW SHAMS TO MATCH

4 FLORAL FABRICS— 1/2 YD. EACH

2 YD. FUSIBLE WEB

SQUEEZE-BOTTLE FABRIC PAINTS—MEDIUM GREEN, LIGHT GREEN, ROSE, PINK AND PEACH

WASHABLE FABRIC GLUE

6 PUSH PINS

BOARD TO PLACE UNDER QUILT ON BED FOR EASY FUSING

CARE REMINDER:
Custom made fused pieces are more delicate and must have special washing care. Hand washing is best, but fused things will tolerate machine washings in cool water. Hang items to air dry. Any fused edges that loosen can be easily secured with washable fabric glue.

STEP 1

Iron fusible web to wrong-side of floral prints, following instructions on inside back cover.

STEP 2

Cut out flower and leaf shapes. This design used 80 floral pieces. Peel away paper backings.

STEP 3

Place board on bed with ironed quilt on top. Place flowers and leaves to form center bouquet encircled by a flower wreath as shown. Fuse designs in place.

STEP 4

Pin quilt to wall for painting ease. Paint around flower and leaf edges with free flowing strokes. Add stems and tendrils with green paints. Allow paint to dry for at least four hours.

Pillow shams: Follow fusing instructions on inside front cover and place flowers as shown.

BLUEBIRD
TOSS PILLOWS

MATERIALS COST: $10-$15   APPROXIMATE TIME TO CREATE: 1/2 HOUR

SUPPLIES

2 READY MADE 14 INCH
SQUARE BEIGE PILLOWS
WITH EMBROIDERED
BORDERS

3 1/2 YD. 1 1/2 INCH WIDE
BEIGE RUFFLED LACE

3 1/2 YD. 4 INCH WIDE BEIGE
RUFFLED LACE

1/4 YD. PRINTED FLORAL
FABRIC WITH BIRDS

1/4 YD. FUSIBLE WEB

SQUEEZE-BOTTLE FABRIC
PAINTS—IRIDESCENT
CHAMPAGNE, PINK, LIGHT
GREEN, MEDIUM GREEN,
AND LILAC

GLUE GUN/GLUE STICKS

Accent your Victorian bed set with soft lace toss pillows. These pillows were purchased at a discount store and embellished with laces, flowers and dear little bluebirds.

STEP 1

Iron fusible web to wrong-side of printed fabrics.

STEP 2

Cut out all flower and leaf shapes. Peel away paper backing.

STEP 3

Fuse flowers and birds in place as shown. Pillows will be more interesting if they do not match exactly.

STEP 4

Paint around birds and flowers with free strokes.

STEP 5

Paint on embroidery details with champagne colored paint, allowing paint to dry completely before adding lace trims.

STEP 6

Glue or stitch 4 inch wide lace around pillow's edge. Add smaller lace on top by gluing in place.

TIP: Adding lace trims...Hot glue will hold lace through warm water washing well. Always hang to dry, as glue will not hold through dryer cycle.

VICTORIAN COTTAGE PILLOW

MATERIALS COST: $5-$10   APPROXIMATE TIME TO CREATE: 30 MINUTES

hite linen pillows are perfect accents on a bed or mixed with colored pillows on a chair. Herbs and potpourri can be placed in pillows for scent.

SUPPLIES

1 19 INCH SQUARE READY MADE WHITE LINEN PILLOW WITH LACE TRIM

1 SQUARE VICTORIAN HOUSE PRINTED COTTON OR ALTERNATE PRINT

1/4 YD. SMALL FLORAL PRINT

1 YD. FUSIBLE WEB

2 YD. 1/4 INCH WIDE PEACH RIBBON

1/2 YD. WIRE EDGE PEACH SILK RIBBON

SQUEEZE-BOTTLE FABRIC PAINTS—BLUE, PEACH AND GREEN

SAFETY PIN

CARE REMINDER:

Custom made fused pieces are more delicate and must have special washing care. Hand washing is best, but fused things will tolerate machine washings in cool water. Hang items to air dry. Any fused edges that loosen can be easily secured with washable fabric glue.

STEP 1
Follow fusing instructions on inside back cover, fuse Victorian cottage to pillow center. Fuse flower sprigs to form wreath around house. Fuse four individual flowers to pillow corners.

STEP 2
Tie 1/4 inch ribbon in four loop bow, cut streamers evenly. Tie wired ribbon in single bow. Pin bows together to pillow as shown.

TIP: Lace painting is great fun and very easy. Paint lace details with squeeze bottle paints. Paint can be mixed with water and applied with a brush for a soft effect.

QUILT BLOCK TABLE COVER

MATERIALS COST: $10-$15   APPROXIMATE TIME TO CREATE: 1 HOUR

ow wonderful it would be to have time to quilt as our grandmothers did. Quilt effects are easy by simply fusing blocks to a plain cloth. Traditional quilt patterns are perfectly adaptable to fusing. We have chosen simple blocks to allow ample cloth showing through.

SUPPLIES

1 70 INCH ROUND RUFFLED TABLECLOTH

1/2 YD. EACH FOUR SMALL PRINTS TO COORDINATE

1/2 YD. STRIPE CLOTH TO COORDINATE

2 YD. FUSIBLE WEB

6 YD. RUFFLED LACE

LIGHT WEIGHT CARDBOARD

GLUE GUN/GLUE STICKS

STEP 1

Fuse web to wrong-side of fabrics following instructions on inside back cover.

STEP 2

Measure and cut a 2 1/2 inch square of cardboard. Using the square as a template, cut 18 squares of each print. Peel away paper backing.

STEP 3

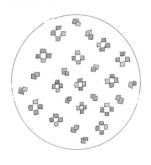

Place cloth on flat surface, position blocks as shown and fuse in place. Skirt gathers will compensate if block spacing is slightly uneven.

STEP 4

Add lace trim to hem ruffle by stitching or with glue gun. If glue is used, cloth may be machine washed in cool water, but must be hung to air dry.

CARE REMINDER:
Custom made fused pieces are more delicate and must have special washing care. Hand washing is best, but fused things will tolerate machine washings in cool water. Hang items to air dry. Any fused edges that loosen can be easily secured with washable fabric glue.

LAMPSHADES BY DESIGN

MATERIALS COST: $5-$10   APPROXIMATE TIME TO CREATE: 45 MINUTES

prigs of garden flowers give cheer whenever this lamp is turned on. Fusing to a shade is simple. Hold shade in one hand, place one floral design on at a time, and iron gently using the tip of an iron.

SUPPLIES

1 10 INCH WHITE LAMPSHADE

1 1/2 YD. 1 INCH WIDE WHITE RUFFLED CROCHET LACE

1/4 YD. FLORAL COTTON PRINT

1/4 YD. FUSIBLE WEB

SQUEEZE-BOTTLE FABRIC PAINTS—LIGHT GREEN, MEDIUM GREEN, PINK AND PEACH

GLUE GUN/GLUE STICKS

STEP 1

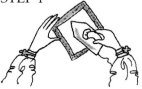

Iron fusible webbing to wrong-side of printed fabric.

STEP 2

Cut out small floral sprigs, peel away paper backing and fuse flowers to shade. Use medium heat setting.

STEP 3

Paint stems and tendrils with green paint. Detail and paint edges of flowers in pink and peach.

STEP 4

Glue lace around top and bottom edge of lamp. Begin at back seam of shade.

VILLAGE CLOTH PICTURE

MATERIALS COST: $5-$15   APPROXIMATE TIME TO CREATE: 1 HOUR

ictorian life included the gentle art of collage. Screens, fans and calling cards were embellished with floral paper scraps.

SUPPLIES

1 RECTANGULAR GOLD PICTURE FRAME (OURS IS 14 BY 25 INCHES)

1 PIECE MEDIUM WEIGHT CARDBOARD CUT TO FIT FRAME

1/4 YD. LIGHT BLUE PRINTED COTTON

1/4 YD. LIGHT GREEN PRINTED COTTON

1/4 YD. WHITE LACE FABRIC

3 SQUARES VICTORIAN HOUSE PRINT ON COTTON OR ALTERNATE PRINT SUITABLE TO SCENE.

SMALL SCRAP FLORAL PRINT—2 SMALL FLOWER SPRAYS

1 1/2 YD. FUSIBLE WEB

SQUEEZE-BOTTLE FABRIC PAINTS TO MATCH PRINT COLORS

FABRIC GLUE

8 PORCELAIN FLOWERS TO COORDINATE WITH PRINT COLORS

GLUE GUN/GLUE STICKS

STEP 1

Iron fusible web to wrong-side of all fabrics except lace, following instructions on inside back cover.

STEP 2

Cut out houses and floral sprigs. Peel away paper backing.

STEP 3

Fuse blue fabric to cardboard to create sky as shown.

STEP 4

Overlap green fabric over blue and fuse in place to create horizon.

STEP 5

Cut out six lace clouds and glue in place using fabric glue.

STEP 6

Fuse houses and flower sprigs as shown.

STEP 7

Paint around design edges, detail picture with paint and add green squiggles for grass effect.

STEP 8

Use glue gun to secure porcelain flowers for a three dimensional garden.

Our Victorian village "painting" is simply an updated expression of this craft.
Inspired by fabric printed with Victorian houses, a lovely
framed piece evolved. Many variations of scenes can originate at the fabric
shop. Mix and match prints to create a wall hanging tailor-made to
your color scheme.

VICTORIAN ROSE WREATH

MATERIALS COST: $25-$30   APPROXIMATE TIME TO CREATE: 1 HOUR

*W*reaths speak of gardens, scents and time gone by. Roses are for special remembrance. Our Victorian rose wreath is a collection of silk, paper, and dried florals for a timeless feeling. Mix your favorite flowers freely to create wreaths for any color scheme. The key to this particular look—roses, pansies and small blossoms all surrounded by emerald leaves, a Victorian posie wreath!

SUPPLIES

1 14 INCH GRAPEVINE WREATH

WARM WATER

63 3 1/2 INCH GREEN SILK ROSE LEAVES

2 LARGE PINK SILK ROSES

1 LARGE BEIGE SILK ROSE

3 STEMS PINK SILK ROSE BUDS

2 STEMS SMALL WHITE SILK BLOSSOMS

2 STEMS SMALL PINK SILK BLOSSOMS

1 STEM MEDIUM WHITE BLOSSOMS

1 STEM SILK LILACS, PINK

1 STEM PEACH PAPER ROSES

1 STEM PINK PAPER ROSES

1 STEM DEEP ROSE PAPER ROSES

1 STEM PAPER PANSIES

1 STEM PINK PAPER SWEET PEAS

4 STEMS DRIED PURPLE LARKSPUR

4 STEMS DRIED PINK LARKSPUR

1 STEM DRIED GERMAN STATICE

GLUE GUN/GLUE STICKS

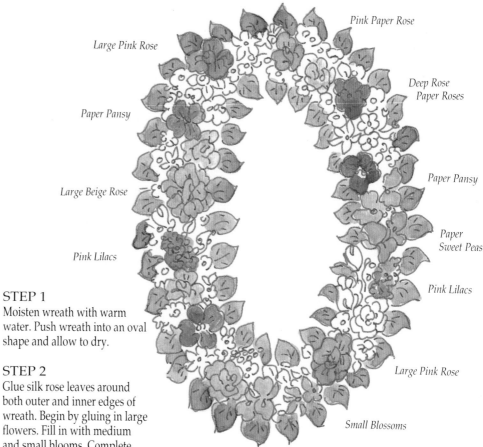

Large Pink Rose

Pink Paper Rose

Paper Pansy

Deep Rose Paper Roses

Large Beige Rose

Paper Pansy

Pink Lilacs

Paper Sweet Peas

Pink Lilacs

Large Pink Rose

Small Blossoms

Paper Sweet Peas

STEP 1
Moisten wreath with warm water. Push wreath into an oval shape and allow to dry.

STEP 2
Glue silk rose leaves around both outer and inner edges of wreath. Begin by gluing in large flowers. Fill in with medium and small blooms. Complete wreath by gluing small sprigs of German statice to soften the look.

STEP 3
Our wreath does not have to be copied exactly for beautiful results, but this diagram shows where focal flowers are placed.

BUNNY BED SET

*R*ich, subtle color works well in a child's room when combined with light walls. Our bed drapings are simply lengths of fabric sewn with a pocket on top and hung on a small curtain rod attached to the wall.

QUILT AND PILLOW COVER SUPPLIES

This project contains a limited amount of sewing for pillow cover.

1 SINGLE PLAIN BED QUILT

1 YD. QUILTED ROSE CALICO PRINT COTTON

1 1/2 YD. ROSE AND CREAM COTTON PILLOW TICKING

1/4 YD. BUNNY PRINT, COTTON

14 INCH SQUARE ROSE CALICO PRINT, UNQUILTED

12 INCH SQUARE ROSE AND CREAM PILLOW TICKING

1 1/4 YD. FUSIBLE WEB

1 1/4 YD. 1/2 INCH BEIGE COTTON LACE TRIM

1/2 YD. EACH ROSE AND BLUE RIBBON—1/4 INCH

1/2 YD. DEEP CRANBERRY RIBBON—1/4 INCH

SMALL SAFETY PIN

GLUE GUN/GLUE STICKS

SEWING MACHINE

PILLOW COVER INSTRUCTIONS

STEP 1

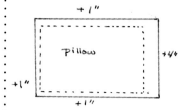

Make a simple pillow cover, following the illustrations above.

STEP 2
Following instructions on inside back cover, fuse three rabbits to pillow cover.

STEP 3

Tie a single bow, using all three ribbon colors and pin bow to pillow as shown. Pinning bow will allow for laundry ease.

BED QUILT INSTRUCTIONS

STEP 1
Fuse web to both 14 inch and 12 inch fabric squares. Cut out heart shapes and fuse calico heart to quilt center, approximately 14 inches below pillow area. Fuse striped heart on calico heart.

STEP 2
Fuse bunnies to heart shapes. Glue or stitch lace trim around heart shapes.

BED DRAPE SUPPLIES

1 ADJUSTABLE CURTAIN ROD

4 1/2 YD. ROSE AND CREAM PILLOW TICKING

4 1/4 YD. ROSE CALICO PRINT, COTTON

10 YD. 3/4 INCH ROSE RIBBON

10 YD. 3/4 INCH BLUE RIBBON

10 YD. 1/2 INCH CRANBERRY RIBBON

GLUE GUN/GLUE STICKS

SEWING MACHINE

STEP 1
Cut calico fabric in half, lengthwise and hem all around edges. Sew a rod pocket on top end of both fabric sections.

STEP 2
Hem stripe fabric all around and sew a rod pocket in top end.

STEP 3
Attach rod to wall, approximately six feet above head of bed. Hang bed curtains as shown, with stripe in center, bordered by calico strips.

STEP 4
Cut five yard lengths of each ribbon color and tie a single bow at center of lengths, using all three ribbons together. Hot glue the bows to calico drape sections and trim ribbon ends.

SUPPLIES FOR TABLE POUF

1 70 INCH WHITE RUFFLED TABLECLOTH

1 1/4 YD. ROSE CALICO PRINT, COTTON

GLUE GUN/GLUE STICKS

2 YD. 1/2 INCH CRANBERRY RIBBON

4 SMALL SAFETY PINS

STEP 1

Fold and glue fabric as shown.

STEP 2

Cut ribbon in four equal lengths and tie as shown.

STEP 3

Pin pouf to tablecloth, under bows.

CARE REMINDER:
Custom made fused pieces are more delicate and must have special washing care. Hand washing is best, but fused things will tolerate machine washings in cool water. Hang items to air dry. Any fused edges that loosen can be easily secured with washable fabric glue.

QUILTED CORNICE

MATERIALS COST: $15-$20   APPROXIMATE TIME TO CREATE: 1 HOUR 15 MINUTES

 *reate custom window treatments inexpensively, using foam core board, fabric and a glue gun. Any unquilted fabric can be substituted, simply pad fabric with cotton batting for a softer effect.*

SUPPLIES

1 LARGE FOAM CORE BOARD

1 SHARP CRAFT BLADE OR KNIFE

NEWSPAPER

GLUE GUN/GLUE STICKS

1 YD. QUILTED ROSE CALICO COTTON

3 YD. 1 INCH BLUE RIBBON

3 YD. 1/2 INCH CRANBERRY RIBBON

1 6 INCH SQUARE LIGHT ROSE CALICO PRINT, UNQUILTED

1 BUNNY CUT FROM PRINTED FABRIC

1 6 INCH SQUARE FUSIBLE WEB

1 SMALL SCRAP FUSIBLE WEB TO COVER BUNNY SHAPE

3/4 YD. 1/2 INCH BEIGE COTTON LACE TRIM

STEP 1
Measure window and decide how deep window cornice is to be. Dimensions of our cornice are 40 inches wide x 11 inches tall x 4 inches deep.

STEP 2
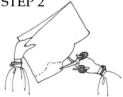

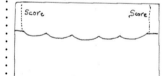

Make a newspaper pattern for bottom edge of cornice. Fold measured newspaper in half to make an even pattern. Draw measurements and pattern on foam core as shown.

STEP 3
Cut foam core board with sharp blade. Score cornice seams completely through board. Do not cut completely through board.

STEP 4

Glue quilted fabric to cornice form as shown.

TIP: Foam core board is extremely light weight...Secure loops to wall with pushpins or small nails.

STEP 5

Fuse web to calico and bunny. Cut a small calico heart. Follow instructions on inside back cover. Fuse heart to cornice as shown. Fuse bunny to heart and glue lace trim around heart with glue gun.

STEP 6

Bend cornice at score marks and reinforce corners by simply gluing a small rectangle of foam core board.

STEP 7

Glue blue ribbon to cornice by wrapping ribbon ends to cornice back and securing with glue. Glue cranberry ribbon to blue ribbon to create a striped effect.

STEP 8

Glue three loops of ribbon to cornice back for hanging purposes.

BUNNY LAMP

MATERIALS COST: $1-$5   APPROXIMATE TIME TO CREATE: 20 MINUTES

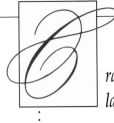

ranberry, blue and rose come alive when this bunny print lampshade is lit. Prints fuse easily to pleated shade.

SUPPLIES FOR BUNNY LAMP

1 10 INCH WHITE PLEATED SHADE

1/8 YD. BUNNY PRINTED COTTON

1/8 YD. FUSIBLE WEB

SUPPLIES FOR BRUSH SET

1 SMALL PINK HAND MIRROR

1 SMALL PINK HAIRBRUSH

1/2 YD. 1 INCH RUFFLED LACE TRIM

30 SMALL GREEN PORCELAIN LEAVES

7 SMALL LAVENDER AND BLUE PORCELAIN FLOWERS

8 SMALL WHITE PORCELAIN FLOWERS

6 SMALL PINK PORCELAIN FLOWERS

5 MEDIUM PINK PORCELAIN ROSES

6 MEDIUM WHITE PORCELAIN ROSES

4 LARGE WHITE PORCELAIN ROSES

1 LARGE PINK PORCELAIN ROSE

1 BUNNY CUT FROM PRINTED FABRIC

CRAFT GLUE

SQUEEZE-BOTTLE FABRIC PAINT—DARK GREEN

GLUE GUN / GLUE STICKS

STEP 1
Following instructions on inside back cover, fuse web to printed fabric. Peel away paper backing and fuse bunnies to shade front.

TIP: Lace, eyelet or ribbons can be used to decorate shades. Fabric paint can be used on ceramic bases for color accents.

BUNNY AND ROSES BRUSH SET

Make this special gift for the young lady you love...Porcelain roses, lace, and of course a little bunny in red shoes, adorn an inexpensive brush set to delight any little girl.

STEP 1

Glue bunny to center on the back of mirror with craft glue.

STEP 2

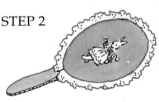

Glue lace trim around mirror's edge with glue gun.

STEP 3

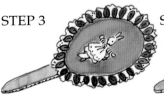

Use glue gun to attach porcelain leaves around mirror's edge.

STEP 4

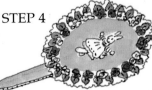

Glue porcelain flowers to mirror as shown.

STEP 5
Paint grass and stem details on mirror with fabric paint.

BRUSH

Simply glue ten porcelain leaves to brush as shown, and glue five porcelain flowers down the center of leaves.

VICTORIAN BASINETTE SET

MATERIALS COST: $10-$15   APPROXIMATE TIME TO CREATE: 1 HOUR

Roses, baby's breath and a sweep of lace for baby's sweet sleep...

SUPPLIES

1 WHITE EYELET BASINETTE SKIRT AND LINER

1/4 YD. ROSEBUD PRINT, COTTON

1/4 YD. FUSIBLE WEB

SQUEEZE-BOTTLE PAINTS—LIGHT PINK, LIGHT ROSE AND MINT GREEN

STEP 1

Following instructions on inside back cover, fuse web to printed fabric.

STEP 2

Cut out rose and leaf shapes. Peel away paper backings.

STEP 3

Fuse designs to basinette skirt. For best effect, the skirt should be on basinette so flowers show on gathers. Simply hold a piece of card under skirt and iron roses in place as shown.

STEP 4

Paint around edges and detail designs with fabric paint.

CARE REMINDER:

Custom made fused pieces are more delicate and must have special washing care. Hand washing is best, but fused things will tolerate machine washings in cool water. Hang items to air dry. Any fused edges that loosen can be easily secured with washable fabric glue.

ROSES AND BABY'S BREATH CROWN

MATERIALS COST: $40-$45   APPROXIMATE TIME TO CREATE: 1 HOUR 30 MINUTES

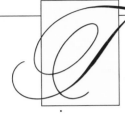

The crowning touch to baby's new room... Roses and baby's breath welcome your new arrival.

SUPPLIES

1 12 INCH EMBROIDERY HOOP, CENTER SECTION

WHITE CRAFT PAINT

12 PINK SILK ROSES AND LEAVES

3 WHITE SILK GARDENIAS

2 STEMS PINK SWEET PEAS

1 BUNCH WHITE BABY'S BREATH

1 SMALL BUNCH WHITE GERMAN STATICE

10 YDS. 1/2 INCH PINK RIBBON

10 YDS. 1/2 INCH PEACH RIBBON

8 YDS. WHITE LACE
the lace used was called "railroad" lace at the fabric shop. It is 32 inches wide and costs under $3.00 per yard!

1 CUP HOOK

STEP 1

Paint embroidery hoop white. Allow paint to dry completely before gluing flowers.

STEP 2

Cut 1 yd. pink ribbon and 1 yd. peach ribbon and tie to hoop as shown. Secure knots around hoop with glue.

STEP 3

Glue roses, gardenias and sweet peas. Fill in between spaces with leaves and dried flowers.

STEP 4

Divide remaining ribbons into two groups, mixing peach with pink and attach to hoop at end of flower sections.

STEP 5

Make a cut down center of lace 1/3 length of lace. Attach cup hook to ceiling above basinette and thread the cut lace over back section of hoop, allowing lace to drape onto floor around basinette sides.

TIP: Adapt our Victorian basinette easily for a boy, by using white roses with a sweep of pastel blue lace or yellow and white roses with blue ribbons.

ROSEBUD AND TEDDY CRIB SET

SEE INDIVIDUAL MATERIALS LISTS FOR TIME AND MATERIALS COSTS.

Baby's crib is complete with a soft eyelet crib quilt and a tiny pillow trimmed with roses and Victorian toys all tied in pretty bows.

SUPPLIES FOR BABY'S QUILT

1 WHITE CRIB QUILT WITH LACE TRIM

1 MATCHING CRIB PILLOW WITH LACE TRIM

1/4 YD. ROSE PRINT, COTTON

1/2 YD. VICTORIAN TOY PRINT, COTTON

1/2 YD. BOW PRINTED COTTON

1 1/2 YD. FUSIBLE WEB

SQUEEZE-BOTTLE FABRIC PAINTS—CRYSTAL GREEN, PINK AND ROSE

MATERIALS COST: $10-$15

APPROXIMATE TIME TO CREATE: 1 HOUR

BABY'S QUILT INSTRUCTIONS

STEP 1

Following instructions on inside back cover, fuse web to printed fabric.

STEP 2

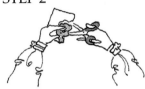

Cut out rose, toy and bow shapes. Peel away paper backings.

STEP 3
Fuse designs to quilt and pillow as shown. Iron well to secure fusing on quilted material.

STEP 4
Paint around edges and detail designs with fabric paint.

CARE REMINDER:
Custom made fused pieces are more delicate and must have special washing care. Hand washing is best, but fused things will tolerate machine washings in cool water. Hang items to air dry. Any fused edges that loosen can be easily secured with washable fabric glue.

DIAPER STORAGE BAG INSTRUCTIONS

SUPPLIES FOR DIAPER STORAGE BAG

1 EYELET DIAPER STORAGE BAG

1/8 YD. ROSE PRINT, COTTON

1 SMALL TOY FROM VICTORIAN PRINT

1/4 YD. FUSIBLE WEB

SQUEEZE-BOTTLE PAINTS— GOLDEN GREEN, PINK AND ROSE

Following the instructions for crib quilt, fuse roses and toy in place and paint edges of design.

NURSERY LAMP

MATERIALS COST: $10-$20   APPROXIMATE TIME TO CREATE: 30 MINUTES

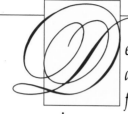

Decorate the nursery lamp with designs used on crib or other accessories for a complete look. Teddy in her pram, was simply fused on a pleated shade with iron on medium setting.

SUPPLIES

1 10 INCH WHITE PLEATED SHADE

1/8 YD. NURSERY PRINT, COTTON

1/8 YD. FUSIBLE WEB

SQUEEZE-BOTTLE FABRIC PAINTS—LIGHT BLUE, PINK AND GREEN

1 SMALL WHITE LAMP— OURS IS NATURAL WOOD, PAINTED WHITE

SILK ROSEBUDS ON RIBBON

GLUE GUN/GLUE STICKS

STEP 1

Following instructions on the inside back cover, fuse web to printed fabric. Peel away paper backing and fuse one design to shade front.

STEP 2

Glue rosebud/ribbon trim to top edge of shade and around lamp base.

STEP 3

Paint dots around lamp base using pink and green paint. Detail fused design with paint.

Fabric paints used to decorate plastics and glass are not permanent through dishwasher cycles, but look so pretty and are so easily renewed...

Simply paint small designs directly on bottles or small accessories. Mistakes can be easily wiped clean with a tissue while paint is still wet. Paint can be peeled away if design is no longer desired.

Paint is for decorative purposes only. Do not allow baby to put painted objects in their mouth.

MOTHER'S ROCKER

MATERIALS COST: $20-$25   APPROXIMATE TIME TO CREATE: 1 HOUR 30 MINUTES

urniture painting has once again come into fashion and is both lovely and easy. Our little rocker was found in a flea market for under $35.00.

SUPPLIES

1 ROCKING CHAIR OR ANY FURNITURE PIECE

DUST CLOTH

3 PIECES FINE SANDPAPER

SMALL TIN/WHITE PRIMER PAINT

BASE COLOR PAINT—ABOUT 8 OZ. COVERED OUR CHAIR

2 INCH PAINT BRUSH

5 OZ. EACH TWO PASTEL COLORS FOR SPONGING

NATURAL SEA SPONGE

SMALL ROSES CUT FROM PRINTED FABRIC

1 SMALL TOY DESIGN CUT FROM PRINTED FABRIC

CRAFT GLUE

1 CAN SATIN SPRAY VARNISH

COLORS USED FOR ROCKER: BASE COLOR—WHITE MIXED WITH A FEW DROPS ROSE TO MAKE PASTEL PINK.

SPONGED COLOR 1—WHITE MIXED WITH FEW DROPS TURQUOISE TO MAKE PALE AQUA.

SPONGED COLOR 1—BASE PASTEL PINK MIXED WITH TEN DROPS DEEP ROSE TO MAKE A DEEPER PASTEL PINK.

Any wood can be painted. The key to painting dark wood is in the primer. Paint stores carry a stain-killer primer that will both seal old wood and prime to a clean white surface, ready for any paint finish.

Painted surfaces, walls, furniture and accessories have a richer, more interesting look, when sponged with two colors over a base color. The third color will give depth to any painted surface.

The steps for painting our rocker are the same for any piece of furniture...

STEP 1
Wipe piece with dust cloth to remove any old soil.

STEP 2
Sand wood lightly and dust away any sawdust.

STEP 3
Prime wood with white primer paint.

STEP 4
Paint wood with base coat. Add a second coat of base color, if needed.

STEP 5
Moisten sponge well and wring out excess water. Dab sponged color one on furniture lightly to create a pattern. Allow paint to dry well.

STEP 6
Follow step five, using the second sponged color.

STEP 7
Glue fabric details to chair. Each piece of furniture will have different design elements. Hold cut outs in different places to see where they look best.

STEP 8
Use a brush to apply larger, solid areas of sponged color. We added stripes and leg details in aqua. If your lines are not perfect, do not worry—simply finish coloring with a light sponging in a second sponge color or base color, as we have done.

STEP 9
Move chair to well ventilated area and spray lightly with satin varnish.

LITTLE ANGEL SHELF

The little angel watches quietly while baby sleeps. Terra cotta angels are available at most craft stores, as are small wooden shelves.

Follow instructions for painted rocker when applying paint. The shelf used leftover paint from chair project.

A small bunch of dried and silk flowers were glued to top of angel's hand. Tiny stems were glued to bottom of hand to give the effect of the angel's hand holding the bouquet.

Angel was glued with hot glue to shelf for safety.

BABY'S RUG

MATERIALS COST: $5-$10   APPROXIMATE TIME TO CREATE: 1 HOUR

SUPPLIES

1 HEART SHAPED CROCHET DOILY

SMALL PAINT BRUSH

SQUEEZE-BOTTLE FABRIC PAINT—PALE YELLOW, PINK AND GREEN

WASHABLE FABRIC GLUE

1 COTTON RAG RUG— OURS IS PINK AND WHITE GINGHAM WEAVE

Baby's first rug combines the homemade feeling of a simple cotton rag rug and the lacy feeling of crochet. Doilies, painted with fabric paint are fun and easy to do.

STEP 1

Moisten doily thoroughly and squeeze out any excess water. Dilute fabric paint with small amount of water on a plate and highlight crochet design areas with color. Painting on a moistened cloth will allow paint to bleed into cloth as if yarns are dyed. Allow doily to dry completely.

STEP 2

Add dots of undiluted fabric paint to design. This paint will show in bolder colors because it will sit on top of fabric—it will not soak in like the diluted paints. Allow paint to dry.

STEP 3
Apply fabric glue to wrong-side of doily and glue in position on center of rug.

STEP 4
Use green paint to draw X marks along rug border.

TIP: A decorated rug is machine washable, on a cool cycle. Design will be protected by air drying rug.

ROSES AND RIBBON BASKET

MATERIALS COST: $5-$10   APPROXIMATE TIME TO CREATE: 20 MINUTES

*R*oses and ribbons of fabric adorn a useful basket for baby's room. Our basket was purchased with plastic liner in a garden shop!

SUPPLIES

1 WHITE WASTEPAPER BASKET

4 OR 5 MEDIUM ROSES WITH LEAVES CUT FROM FABRIC

CRAFT GLUE

1 1/2 YD. COTTON BORDER PRINT

GLUE GUN/GLUE STICKS

STEP 1

Cut flowers with leaves from fabric and glue to center of basket. Press flower shapes onto surface, so glue has complete contact.

STEP 2

Use glue gun to attach cut out border print to top rim of basket.

STEP 3

Make a single bow with remaining border fabric and hot glue to basket just above roses.

TIP: Fabric paints may be used to detail flowers and leaves.

TIP: Decorate small baskets to hang on the wall for small item storage.

PINK VIOLETS BATH SET

MATERIALS COST FOR EACH PROJECT $5-$10   APPROXIMATE TIME TO CREATE (EACH) 20 MINUTES

*B*athrooms need not be neglected. Create lovely bath accessories easily and inexpensively...

Bath towels, pillows and bath rugs have all been decorated with pink chintz violets. A skirted table has been topped with a hemmed square of the print used for applique.

SUPPLIES REMAIN CONSTANT FOR ALL THREE PROJECTS

1/4 YD. FLORAL VIOLET CHINTZ

1/4 YD. FUSIBLE WEB

SQUEEZE BOTTLE FABRIC PAINTS—GREEN, PINK AND ROSE

CARE REMINDER:

Custom made fused pieces are more delicate and must have special washing care. Hand washing is best, but fused things will tolerate machine washings in cool water. Hang items to air dry. Any fused edges that loosen can be easily secured with washable fabric glue.

STEP 1

Following illustrations of inside back cover, fuse web to reverse-side of print.

STEP 2

Cut out flower and leaf shapes. Peel away paper backing.

STEP 3

Iron flower and leaf shapes in place on towels, rugs or pillows.

STEP 4

Outline shapes with free flowing strokes.

PAINTED LACE
AND
EMBROIDERY

hite on white embroidery and lace is easily brought to life with pastel fabric paints.

Peach, rose and light green craft paints, mixed with water and applied with a small craft brush bleed into cotton, giving a soft dyed effect (One part paint to six parts water).

PAINTED LACE SHELF SKIRT
Glue 5 inch deep, ruffled, embroidered cotton around front and side edges of a small wooden wall shelf. Pink, rose and green craft paint, mixed with a small amount of water and applied to embroidery with a small paint brush, finish the look.

GUEST TOWELS
Simply, paint dots of color using a small paint brush. Water paints slightly and apply dots to French knots on embroidered guest towels.

VICTORIAN POTPOURRI

ictorian rooms, gently scented with garden and spice perfumes...china bowls brimming with potpourri greeted guests, fragrance of quiet times fill the air...

Creating potpourri is much like cooking or gardening—a blending of colors, textures and scents. Potpourri recipes are really guidelines—follow carefully or experiment. Once you make potpourri, you will become enchanted by the endless possibilities.

Potpourri extends the joy of a gardener's year. Collect flowers, petals and leaves throughout the year to be mixed during the autumn as fresh flowers fade.

Health food shops have selections of dried herbs and flowers in bulk. Craft stores have good selections of dried materials and both stores will have scented oils for potpourri use.

FIXATIVES

Essential, or scented, oils give potpourri fragrance. Mixed into dried materials without a fixative, the scent will soon fade. Orris root is the dried, crushed root of an iris. It is especially absorbent and when mixed with oils, it acts like a sponge—holding fragrance for a long time.

Flowers from the home garden are perfect for potpourri. Pick flowers and leaves on a dry day, after dew has evaporated. Tie in small bunches and hang on pegs, or dry material flat on screens in a warm place, away from direct light.

Herbs, Spices and Flowers suitable for drying...

HERBS

Bay, Bergamot, Borage, Catmint, Chamomile, Lemon Balm, Lemon Verbena, Marjoram, Mint, Parsley, Pennyroyal, Rosemary, Sage, Scented Geraniums, Tansy, Tarragon, Thyme, Yarrow

SPICES

Allspice, Aniseed, Cinnamon, Cloves, Corriander, Ginger, Nutmeg, Mace, Star Anise

FLOWERS

Alyssum, Aster, Baby's Breath, Bergamot, Calendula, Carnations, Cornflower, Daisy, Delphinium, Forget-me-not, Geranium, Honeysuckle, Hydrangea, Jasmine, Larkspur, Lavender, Lilac, Lobelia, Mallow, Marigold, Pansy, Pinks, Rose, Salvia, Statice, Sunflower, Veronica, Violet, Wallflower, Yarrow, Zinnia.

ESSENTIAL OILS

Lavender, rose, lilac, and dozens of floral and exotic oils await you. Use oils in single drops until the blend pleases you. Always mix potpourri in china or glass bowls.

Freshen tired potpourri with the addition of orris root scented with additional oil. It is natural for a bowl of potpourri to need freshening up. The delight of making potpourri is its ability to last for years with only the small addition of occasional oil.

ENGLISH ROSE POTPOURRI

MATERIALS COST: $5-$10   APPROXIMATE TIME TO CREATE: 20 MINUTES

*A*waken in a beautiful Victorian bedroom filled with the scent of a rose garden after a summer's rain. Scent is the finishing touch to any room, and so easy and delightful to make. Potpourri, pronounced po-purr-ee, is a mixture of dried petals and spices kept in jars and bowls for its perfume. Color, texture and scent are all part of the magic of potpourri. This recipe was given to me by a dear friend in England.

RECIPE FOR ENGLISH ROSE POTPOURRI

4 OZ. ROSE PETALS

1 OZ. ORANGE PEEL

1 OZ. MARJORAM

1 OZ. BAY LEAVES

4 TBS. LAVENDER

4 TBS. LEMON VERBENA

6 TBS. BLUE CORNFLOWERS

2 TBS. CRUSHED CINNAMON STICKS

2 TBS. CRUSHED CLOVES

2 TBS. DRIED GREEN LEAVES

4 TBS. ORRIS ROOT

18 DROPS ROSE OIL

5 DROPS ORANGE OIL

Mix orris root with rose and orange oil in large glass or china bowl. Add all dried materials and mix well, be sure colors are well distributed. Place potpourri in a plastic bag, twist tie bag and store for three weeks to allow petals and leaves to become well scented. Freshen tired potpourri with additional scented orris root for stronger room scent.

ROSE POMANDER

MATERIALS COST: $5-$10
APPROXIMATE TIME TO
CREATE: 20 MINUTES

SUPPLIES

1 GLASS POMANDER BALL

1/4 YD. CORD TRIM

1/2 YD. GINGHAM RIBBON

7 DRIED ROSEBUDS

DRIED BABY'S BREATH

PINK TASSLE

GLUE GUN/GLUE STICK

Fill pomander with English rose potpourri. Secure cord to top opening with glue gun. Tie cord as shown and glue two gingham bows to cord. Glue rosebuds and baby's breath just above bow. Glue pink tassle as shown.

Glass pomander balls look like clear Christmas ornaments, but have tiny holes on the ball's surface.

Fill a pomander ball with English rose potpourri. Use a glue gun to secure cord and tassle to glass ball.

LAVENDER POTPOURRI

MATERIALS COST: $5-$10   APPROXIMATE TIME TO CREATE: 20 MINUTES

*E*nglish lavender makes the most simple, beautiful potpourri. French lavender blossoms are larger and more delicately scented. Blend a few pink rose petals for color.

RECIPE FOR ENGLISH LAVENDER POTPOURRI

3 OZ. DRIED ENGLISH LAVENDER

6 OR 7 DRIED ROSE LEAVES, GENTLY BROKEN

PINK ROSE PETALS— TWO DRIED PINK ROSES WILL DO

1 TBS. ORRIS ROOT

6 DROPS LAVENDER OIL

Mix orris root with lavender oil in a large glass or china bowl. Gently, mix lavender, rose leaves and petals with scented orris root.

Place potpourri in prepared, brown paper bag. Secure folded top with clothespin and allow potpourri to season for two to three weeks.

LAVENDER POTPOURRI BUNNY

MATERIALS COST: $5-$10
APPROXIMATE TIME TO CREATE: 20 MINUTES

SUPPLIES

1 PAPER MACHE BUNNY FORM

CRAFT GLUE

WAXED PAPER

2 CUPS LAVENDER POTPOURRI

1 YD. 1/2 INCH CRANBERRY RIBBON

Working on waxed paper, cover bunny with craft glue. Pour potpourri on waxed paper and roll glue covered bunny to cover with potpourri. Allow time for glue to dry and patch any missed places with more glue and potpourri. Tie a pretty bow around bunny's neck.

VICTORIAN KITCHEN POTPOURRI

 *itchens scented with herbs, spices and citrus, delight the senses before baking even begins!*

VICTORIAN KITCHEN POTPOURRI RECIPE

1 OZ. DRIED
ORANGE PEEL

3 OZ. LEMON VERBENA
LEAVES

3 OZ. CALENDULA
PETALS—ALSO KNOWN
AS POT MARIGOLD

1 OZ. CLOVES

1/2 OZ. SWEET
MARJORAM

1 TBS. ORRIS ROOT

10 DROPS
ORANGE OIL

5 DROPS VANILLA

Mix orris root with scented oils in large glass or china bowl. Add all dried materials and mix well, using gentle motions. Be sure colors are well distributed. Scents of orange and vanilla will rise around you. Place potpourri in prepared, brown paper bag and secure folded top with a clothespin. Allow to season for two to three weeks.

POTPOURRI IDEAS...

• *Scent cards and letters by adding a pinch of potpourri just before sealing envelope.*

• *Potpourri in small toss pillows helps scent the room.*

• *Toss potpourri in bottom of lingerie drawer.*

• *Cut circles of lace fabric, add a handful of potpourri and tie with a pretty ribbon.
Tie ribbon loop around hanger to scent closet.*

• *Place potpourri in storage boxes to keep things fresh.*

VICTORIAN SPICE POTPOURRI

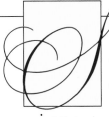

picy, herbal, potpourris scent the dining room with fragrance complimentary to food. Experiment with dried leaves, petals and spices, or try my Victorian Spice potpourri.

VICTORIAN SPICE POTPOURRI RECIPE

1 OZ. LEMON VERBENA LEAVES	1/2 OZ. RED CLOVER	1/2 OZ. POWDERED CINNAMON
3 OZ. ROSE HIPS	1/2 OZ. ROSEMARY	1 TBS. ORRIS ROOT
3 OZ. SANDALWOOD	1/2 OZ. DRIED ORANGE PEEL	15 DROPS LAVENDER OIL
1 OZ STRAWBERRY LEAVES		

Mix orris root with lavender oil in a large glass or china bowl. Add dried materials and mix gently. Place potpourri in a prepared, brown paper bag and secure folded top with clothespin. Season potpourri for two to three weeks.

POTPOURRI WALL SACHET

MATERIALS COST: $5-$10
APPROXIMATE TIME TO CREATE: 20 MINUTES

SUPPLIES

1 SMALL WHITE SACHET PILLOW

1 YD. 1 3/4 INCH VARIEGATED RIBBON

5 DRIED PINK ROSES

3 DRIED WHITE ROSES

BABY'S BREATH

GLUE GUN/GLUE STICK

Potpourri sachets can adorn walls or be hung in closets to freshen and scent clothing. Sachets placed in the linen closet make for delightful dreams.

Fill sachet pillow with potpourri. Cut ribbon in half. Glue sachet to flat ribbon section two inches from top. Tie a double bow and glue to ribbon top. Glue roses and baby's breath just below bow. Trim ribbon.

CREATING
COLOR SCHEMES

olor is the most inexpensive of luxuries. There are no hard and fast rules about color but creating harmony in a room is largely dependent on the colors you choose. Color is affected by many elements in a room. Shadow, light, time of day and other colors all affect the color selected for walls, fabrics, accessories and floors. Where to begin?

The first step is to determine which colors you really want to live with. Certain colors lift the spirit, others make us feel low. If you have ever dressed in the morning and had to change because it just did not feel right to wear that color, then you know exactly how we are affected by color. Surround yourself with colors you feel comfortable with.

Victorian rooms usually incorporate printed fabrics, and what better place to start! The selection of a print is a very personal choice. Clipping photos of rooms you love from magazines will offer a good idea of the prints you enjoy. Your local fabric shop is brimming with prints and color ideas. When in doubt, purchase small amounts of several prints you like and take them home to test in your room.

Here is our main print.

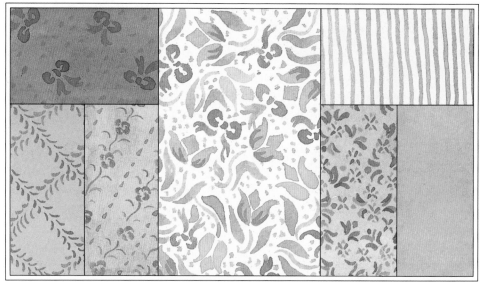

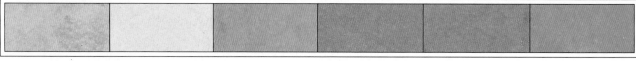

Here are the individual colors used in our print.

BUILDING A COLOR SCHEME AROUND A PRINT

Choose a floral print that pleases you and will work well for the time of day you use the room. If you had chosen the print above, how could color schemes develop?

You can attain harmony by using colors and patterns to coordinate. Smaller prints, stripes, plain fabrics and accessories will accent your chosen print. Pastels, or whitened tones of a color used in the main print will make walls a perfect backdrop for your setting.

CRAFT AND
DECORATING TIPS

*V*ictorian home applique projects can be accomplished three ways. Stitching fabric cut outs by hand or by machine is the classic method. Washable fabric glues are a second option. These glues do hold well through cool washings and air drying. The third method as described in our project instructions is fusing. I have found fusing to be a most effective craft technique, as I am, unfortunatetly a non-sewer.

NO SEW TECHNIQUE

You will need...paper backed fusible web or sheets, printed fabric, sharp scissors, an iron.

1. Iron fusible to wrong-side of fabric.

2. Cut design, peel away paper backing.

3. Iron design onto item.

4. Secure design edges by simply painting with squeeze bottle fabric paints, or stitching. Fused edges hold well if care instructions are closely followed.

PAINTING ON FABRICS

Fabric paints are now available in pearlized, iridescent, and glittering finishes, as well as flat and shiny.

Always allow at least four hours drying time, so paint dries completely before item is used.

Paints can be applied directly from small squeeze bottles, or with a small brush.

Fabric paints are acrylic, and water base, and can be mixed with water for color washes. Test all paints on a small fabric scrap for best results.

Tiny beads or dots of pearlized cream or white paint, will give the effect of pearls. Dot paint around edge of applique for a beaded effect.

NOTIONS USEFUL IN HOME DECORATING CRAFTS

Tassles, Pearls, Flat Lace, Ruffled Lace, Battenburg Lace, Woven Ribbon, Wire Edged Ribbon, Small Silk Flowers, Small Silk Leaves, Tiny Pom-poms, Gold braids and trim, Glass Buttons, Embroidery Floss, Fringe Trim, Cording, Jewel Trims.

EASY, INEXPENSIVE — CRAFT PROJECTS FOR

THE VICTORIAN HOME

By Joni Prittie

Beautiful rooms, accented with easily created, Victorian inspired accessories... Everything you need to know to decorate your home with an updated Victorian feeling. Each project includes time and cost information. Decorate with the joy of creating and saving.

MARK
PUBLISHING

5400 SCOTTS VALLEY DR.
SCOTTS VALLEY, CA 95066

ISBN 0-937769-81-9